YOGA for SUITS

YOGA for SUITS

30 No-Sweat Power Poses to Do in Pinstripes

by Edward Vilga

RUNNING PRESS
PHILADELPHIA · LONDON

9 8 7 6 5 4 3 2 1

Digit on the right indicates the number of this printing

Library of Congress Control Number: 200692853

ISBN-13: 978-0-7624-2621-8
ISBN-10: 0-7624-2621-7

Cover and interior design by Corinda Cook
Edited by Sheridan Deborah Grandinetti
Photo Shoot directed by Edward Vilga
Photography by David Plakke (www.davidplakke.com)
Models: Cristy Candler and Tracy James
Suit worn by Tracy James by DKNY
Typography: Avenir and Baskerville

This book may be ordered by mail from the publisher. Please include $2.50 for postage and handling.
But try your bookstore first!

Running Press Book Publishers
125 South Twenty-second Street
Philadelphia, Pennsylvania 19103-4399

Visit us on the web!
www.runningpress.com

Contents

Disclaimer

Although the yoga poses in this book are designed to be gentle and appropriate for almost everyone, the author and publisher advise readers to know their physical limits and take full responsibility for their own well-being. As with any exercise program, get your doctor's approval before beginning.

To all my students, teachers, friends, and supporters, especially:

Dana Flynn and Jasmine Tarkeshi for creating an awesome community at the Laughing Lotus, for offering me the permission to be myself, and for giving me unbelievable opportunities to share that adventure.

David Plakke for once again taking sensational photographs, being a pleasure to work with, and demonstrating the patience of a saint.

Cristy Candler—yoga model and friend extraordinaire—for never settling for less than fabulous and for being continuously available for the next reshoot. Tracy James was an ideal partner for her and a total pro to have on board.

Deborah Grandinetti and Running Press for believing in this project and *Yoga in Bed*.

Corinda Cook for braving New York City for the photo shoot and approving every detail.

Emma Sweeney in gratitude for her continued support and for the joy of working with such a classy professional.

Lisa Lori, Lori Diamond, and Patricia Rallis, who are a publicity Dream Team.

Roger Gonzalez whose work with S.E.S.A.M.E. is inspiring enough, but who has also taken friendship, support, and faith to a new level.

Fara Marz for his spirited support, particularly the use of his beautiful Om Factory (www.omfactorynyc.com) for our photo shoot.

Joanna Candler, David Tine, Stephen Anderson, Rosemarie Bria (and Midgie), Alnoor Kassam, David McMahon, Karen Lindskog, Alana Newhouse, and Doug Claney for jumping on the yoga bandwagon and making the journey forward possible.

Erik J. Auli for crackerjack assistance on this project and others.

Stacey Lynn Brass, Hillary Kelleher, Patty Kelly, and Jennifer Brian—amazing teachers and wonderful friends who greatly strengthened this manuscript with their thoughtful comments.

Adam Mastrelli, Anne Marie Bradley, Autumn Saville, all of whom I want on every film experience I have. For this shoot, Janice Rogers for wardrobe and Maria Tandecreti for make-up. Both did excellent work.

Bryn Chrisman for her sensational blend of yoga glamour and generosity.

Dan Segan for endless computer consulting and being my "No" Guy.

Friends who've been there through thick and thin: Amy Adler, Nicole Bettauer, Genevieve Lynch, and Chris Ryan.

Leslie Lewis Sword for awesome support, friendship, and sharing the journey of spirit.

Douglas Boyce for the guardian angel generosity behind all his referrals.

Alecia Cohen and Jon Chaloner for helpful inspirations.

Terrence McNally for his spirited inversions.

Patricia Scanlon and Hugh Palmer, my first students.

My immediate family: Edward and Helen Vilga and Aunt Gen; The Careys—Mary and Tom, and my nephews and niece Brendan, Rachel and Ian; The Krenickys—Carol and Peter, and Elizabeth and William; David and Elizabeth Vilga, and their children Michael, Lauren, and Blake. (And while I'm at it, a shout out to Atherton Phleger, my San Francisco godchild, and the whole Phleger family: Peter, Courtney, Harley, and Tilman.)

Finally, to all the Suits I've taught in my yoga career, and who in turn, have taught me far more.

MY YOGA MEMO

Why Yoga for Suits?

In my New York City practice, I find that most of my private clients are "Suits:" corporate types who have climbed the ladder of success brilliantly, but are usually in desperate need of stretching.

I love teaching these Suits, and make it clear to all of them all that yoga needs to be a steady, frequent, and (ideally) daily practice.

You wouldn't dream of eating only once a week, or brushing your teeth a couple of times a month whenever you manage to squeeze it in. Just like meals and flossing, a little yoga needs to become incorporated into your day.

That's why *Yoga for Suits* shows the poses in the setting where you'll actually practice them: the office itself.

But Yoga for Suits? Is That Possible?

Yoga isn't just for people who live in caves. Nor does it require wearing a loincloth, covering yourself in ashes, or withdrawing from the world. It's also for those of us with student loans and/or mortgage payments to pay, even our own kids in college with hefty tuition bills. In fact, it's really when you're in the thick of things—navigating the corporate jungle, negotiating with clients, or stuck in traffic on your way to a major meeting—that you most need the calming benefits of yoga.

Yoga helps you stay centered and, when you stray from that place, to return to it more quickly. The poses I teach you in this book comprise a practical "yogic tool kit." They can help you tune up your mind/body/spirit when life throws you off balance. Since the modern workplace is particularly adept at that, why not use this ancient, time-honored system to re-balance yourself, so you can be your best no matter what conditions you face? *Yoga for Suits* can give you the edge you need to succeed.

The Business of Yoga

To make it relevant for you modern business types, I designed the *Yoga for Suits* workout to be **IMMEDIATE, ACCESSIBLE, REALISTIC,** and **EFFECTIVE.**

IMMEDIATE: Whenever you feel like it, take a moment and try one of these straight-forward poses, breathing exercises, or meditations. Almost everything in the book can be done at your desk with minimal fuss. You don't have to use any special props, change your clothes, or shower afterward. When you're done, it's back to work, but with a clearer mind and more relaxed body!

ACCESSIBLE: With the modifications I have suggested throughout, practically every pose is doable by any healthy individual. Just be sensitive to your body's range of motion. Don't force anything.

REALISTIC: Many executives, especially those who travel often, simply don't have the time for longer classes or workouts. But truthfully, everyone—even the busiest CEO or the most harried assistant—can integrate a handful of stretches and soothing breaths into his or her day.

Finally, *Yoga for Suits* is enormously **EFFECTIVE**. In the short term, it can free up tight hamstrings, hunched-over shoulders, cranky necks, and frazzled brains. Over time, the benefits get even better. If you do these poses frequently as part of your workday, your body *will* "open up." And while you may never become limber enough to get your feet behind your head, greater flexibility, toning, and stress relief are guaranteed.

A regular practice can lower your heart rate and blood pressure. The flexibility you gain can immeasurably enhance your well-being. It will also help you develop the stamina and endurance you need to achieve real success.

Yoga for Greater Productivity

Although caffeine can jolt you awake, it can also leave your mind feeling frenzied. Yoga, on the other hand, can revitalize you, while leaving your mind calm and clear. Having a sense of calm during the workday is a tremendous boon. The clearer your mind, the easier it is to do good work and make good choices. Everyone is more effective when relaxed. Even beyond that, the relaxation you radiate has a positive affect on everyone

around you, which benefits all of your relationships. Working with the body through yoga can clear the mind, help you reconnect with your spirit, and make your interactions with everyone on your path a lot more peaceful.

The Yoga of Business

Yoga involves more than just poses. It's informed by a philosophy that addresses every aspect of life. Yoga has a very broad code of ethics—the *Yamas* and *Niyamas*—which is pretty straightforward but also very open to personal adaptation. For example, non-violence, non-stealing, and truthfulness are among the concepts it advocates.

Each person has to interpret how these principles fit into his or her own personal and professional life. Obviously, stealing as defined by the law would be wrong by anyone's standard. But it's important that you look inside to make sure you're not stealing by taking advantage of others in more subtle ways. An unfair deal, for example, might legally make you some extra profit, but isn't consistent with higher standards of behavior.

Modern life seems increasingly complicated, and there may be situations, especially at work, where you need to operate within a pre-existing system that's less than ideal. You may not be a revolutionary—or want to move to that mountaintop commune—but it's important that you uncover a way of living that's consistent with your standards.

Work presents an excellent opportunity to do just that: to uncover your values in a world that can present a lot of conflicting options. The competing demands of your environment, however frustrating they sometimes seem, give you the greatest possibility to make choices. The truer you stay to your evolving sense of right behavior, the greater your peace of mind and the happier your life will be.

GETTING TO THE BOTTOM LINE

What Is Yoga?
Yoga (or Yogurt) in the Office*

* Everything you always wanted to know about yoga but were afraid to ask

In this new millennium, nearly everyone's heard about yoga, yet many people are still confused. Some people even wonder about the yoga/yogurt connection (there is none; both words just begin with "Yo").

So before I launch into the specifics of *Yoga for Suits*, here's some basic information about the Big Picture of what yoga is and how it can improve your life.

Exactly what is yoga? Is it a religion?

First of all, yoga is a philosophy, not a religion.

It doesn't require adopting any new religious beliefs, just exploring the concepts of letting go, acceptance, and staying present.

The goal of yoga according to the most ancient texts is "to calm the storms of the mind." In other words, finding a quality of peace and happiness in our lives. That's a goal that's hard to argue with and is of tremendous benefit to anyone. The more high-pressured your professional life is, the more you need to weave a little yoga into it.

In business especially, one wants a calm, cool mind. In almost any office situation—from an intense meeting, to dealing with a difficult client, to maintaining a standard of excellence on the job—the advantages of clearheadedness are obvious.

Where does yoga come from?

Yoga originated over 5,000 years ago in India. The oldest writings—the *Yoga Sutras* and the *Upanishads*—date from this time.

Yet yoga is not a rigid system, nor is it carved in stone. It evolves and grows with many different styles as people constantly develop and explore the practice.

So is yoga just doing poses like in a gym class?

No, yoga is far more than just doing physical poses in the gym. Although this is part of the practice, to really explore yoga means not just to stretch, but also to travel a highly ethical path, while pursuing breathing and centering meditation.

For many people, the physical practice is a first and major step. The body opens, and tensions start to dissolve in the muscles and in the soul. But while just stretching is a very good thing, the universe of yoga—especially the possibility of finding more joy in your life—offers so much more.

So what is the point of yoga poses?

The physical poses are designed to promote good health and release tension in the body, so you can have a peaceful mind and a happy life.

They have been developed and adapted by many different yoga masters over the centuries so that almost anyone can approach them and derive tremendous health benefits.

How's it different from working out?

Yoga isn't just another "workout," however. It's not approached with a conventional workout spirit. Teachers try to share the physical poses along with the philosophical ideas that bring calm and centering. Good yoga classes encourage self-acceptance, non-competition, and gentleness in poses rather than pushing and getting aggressive.

In the same way, more and more, new business models speak about synergies and healthy approaches to competition that can create success stories without negative side effects. Businesses that rely on a win-lose mindset, while they may be profitable, are proving less and less attractive. Parallel to this, more and more people are striving for balanced lives, rather than ones that are unsatisfying despite all the trophies associated with business success.

How does that apply to the physical "workout" part of yoga?

Another major difference from working out is that when practicing any pose, we're perhaps even more interested in what's going on inside the mind than we are in the body.

Correct alignment is absolutely important so that the mind/body connection can help you to de-stress naturally. But perhaps more than this, slowing down and watching the breath allows you to develop a different, improved relationship with your own thoughts and feelings.

In other words, the workout is both interior and exterior, physical and mental.

Who can do yoga?

Anyone of any age or any fitness level can enjoy yoga.

I've taught yoga to everyone from elementary school kids to retirees. All that's required is a willingness to learn—and have fun!

Not everyone can do the same things, of course.

It's important to know your limits. For example, if you have serious health problems, or lower back issues, or even if you're healthy and happily pregnant, than not every pose in this book is necessarily right for you. Nonetheless, after speaking with your doctor, there will definitely be some version of yoga that you can do.

As an example, standing on your head is a fantastic yoga pose, but not possible for everyone. Most folks, however, can do Getting a Leg Up (page 98) which offers many of the same benefits but with far fewer challenges. Although seemingly miles apart from each other, both poses are inversions that revitalize the system.

With a little creativity, and the right information, you will learn how to adapt any pose appropriately to exactly where you are right now.

Are there are different kinds of yoga?

Yes, there are many different styles and flavors of yoga. Although they all have things in common and poses usually overlap, classes might feel and look very different.

For example, some classes such as Ashtanga or Vinyasa, move flowingly. They emphasize coordinating the breath while moving from pose to pose.

Others are Iyengar-influenced and might involve holding only a couple of poses, focusing on detailed alignment, and working extremely specifically.

Restorative classes use props to let the body hold a shape and open deeply and slowly.

There are yoga practices like Kundalini in which certain types of vigorous breathing and simple repetitive motions are more strongly emphasized. There are even newer-style classes these days (like Bikram) taking place in heated rooms because some people feel it opens the muscles up dramatically.

And of course there are classes like Yoga-Mamas or Yoga Seniors and those that address other specific health concerns.

Part of the beauty of yoga is that it's so highly adaptable. With a little exploration, you're bound to find the practice that really speaks to you.

Why should I do yoga?

Yoga helps with:

- Flexibility

- Deep relaxation

- Feeling "centered"

- Strength building

- Cleansing internal organs (detoxifying)

- Improving circulation

- Balance and coordination

- Healing and restoring the body's natural metabolism

- Happiness and a general sense of well-being

These are things that can benefit anyone and everyone.

And in the workplace, having a better attitude, experiencing less stress, and having greater focus can bring tremendous professional and personal benefits.

Particularly as we grow older, the physical practice of yoga can help us increase and sustain flexibility without some of the harsher side effects of other workouts.

Is there anything "weird" about yoga?

Not really.

Some of it might be new, however, and you could encounter a bit of a learning curve. I've taught many successful executives who run global empires but aren't connected to their own breath and bodies. Sometimes they start yoga and feel a bit like fish out of water, but then quickly begin to adjust and succeed quite rapidly. Many of the skills that propelled them up the corporate ladder—commitment, intelligence, and a willingness to learn—translate brilliantly into yoga breakthroughs.

But all in all, there's nothing at all odd or radical about any of the practices and ideas presented in *Yoga for Suits*.

How long does it take to "get good" at yoga?

Bear in mind that "Getting good" doesn't mean mastering difficult poses.

Someone can practice yoga for years, developing much better health and greater peace of mind, without ever bending themselves into a pretzel. Everyone is different, and all measures of progress have to be evaluated individually. While it's exciting to have students experience breakthroughs—today I touched my toes!—what's truly gratifying is the increased awareness you have of your body and an overall feeling of greater contentment in your life. All of this translates into being a happier, more productive person.

How long does this take?

Even a single yoga session can teach you something about the body and the mind, although a steady practice is required to really get the greatest benefits. The most important thing is just getting started!

MORNING MOVES

Every morning is a chance to begin our journey again.

   With all of these poses, take a few moments to reinvigorate the body, to open things up physically, and most importantly, to refresh your attitude as the day begins.

Power-On Meditation

Instead of just plunking down in your chair and plunging into work, give yourself a few moments as you turn on the computer to do your own personal "Power-On" for the day.

While your computer goes through all its restart motions, make sure that you're "restarting" as well.

Try to view the day ahead with fresh eyes. Don't focus on yesterday's difficulties or what's looming ahead on your monthly planner. Instead, as your computer is revving up, make sure you

realize that today is an entirely different day from yesterday. Allow the possibility of a fresh attitude—a personal "restart" if you will—through a few centering deep breaths before you tackle any work.

In yoga, we inhale and exhale through the nose, letting the belly fill up on the inhale. It's the easy, natural way that a baby breathes, but we adults often forget. (How often have you held your breath during a tense conference call?) In pose after pose in *Yoga for Suits*, I'll remind you that the breath is at the center of the yoga practice. There's no better time to establish a good breathing practice than during your powering-on, morning restart.

As you bring your awareness to your breath, decide on your personal focus for the day. Spend a few moments visualizing what effect you want to create in the world, beyond what you have to accomplish and what your boss and staff expect from you.

In the end, most of what needs to be accomplished, will get done—it's the attitude and spirit behind the work that matters most.

No matter what your job, you and your work touch many more lives than you realize. Restarting for two minutes each morning while watching the breath—combined with the right, positive attitude—will profit you, your company, and everyone with whom you work.

Benefits:

Your computer is a powerful tool to gather your thoughts, record your experiences, and communicate with the world. Your mind is even more powerful at these tasks.

Everyone knows that simply turning off computers, copy machines, or printers for a moment and then turning them back on can sometimes solve the problem. So any time machinery jams up, or computers crash, or any personal miscommunication happens, take advantage of this unscheduled "time-out" to breathe deeply, and re-boot your mind.

Throughout the day, whenever you restart your computer (or just need a personal restart), use your breath to regroup until you feel and radiate peace and positive energy. The energy will ripple out in ways you may never know, but the world will feel.

Try it. Take ten, or even just five full breaths and see if everything in your life doesn't come "back on line" a little clearer and cleaner.

It's an interesting paradox. Instead of pushing harder, sometimes the best way to move forward is to take a step back and quietly reflect.

Upward Spiral

In business, profits spiraling upward are a good thing.

In yoga, twisting releases the spine, allowing energy to spiral upward in the body—also a very good thing.

Sit on the forward part of your desk chair.

One hand reaches for the opposite knee (or the outside of the opposite leg).

The other hand reaches for the back of your chair.

Get really tall as you breathe in. Feel the heart lift. Try to remember to do this on each and every inhale.

As you exhale, twist toward the back of the chair.

Let your neck stay relaxed, as your shoulder blades meet on your

back, and your heart lifts. You might even dip the chin down a bit toward the chest so that there's no strain in the neck. You're trying to have most of the movement come from the belly. It's as though you could bring the navel in the direction you're twisting toward.

Stay for a few breaths in this pose, letting yourself twist a little deeper on the exhale, and releasing a little bit on the inhale. See if by going in and out of the twist very, very slightly, you can gently open deeper into it.

After a moment, inhale as you come back to center. Then journey over to the other side.

Benefits:

Start out the day sitting tall! Working out the kinks in the spine while lengthening it is a fantastic way to begin your day. As though you were a sponge, let twisting wring all the worry from your body.

Yogis know that twists help cleanse internal organs in the body, detoxifying and revitalizing your system. (Twisting is great anytime, but you might find it particularly helpful to filter out a three-martini lunch or that late-night office celebration.)

The dialogue you're establishing with your breath—lengthening tall on the inhale and twisting more deeply on the exhale—establishes a pattern of moving consciously that will serve you throughout all your daily dealings. Adding mind/body awareness—especially through the breath connection—allows everything you do to have that yogic calm.

Attitude Elevator

Sit comfortably on the front part of your chair's seat.

Bring your hands behind you, letting your fingers rest on the back part of your chair. Palms are down, with the fingers pointing away.

Breathe in, lifting your heart-center skyward. This will make your arms longer and straighter. You'll feel your shoulder blades moving together on your back.

When you exhale, the chest will soften down a bit, but you'll notice that it feels more open and stretched. As with all yoga *asanas* (poses), the opening you've created will last beyond the time spent in the pose.

With continued practice, you'll reset your body's defaults so that more and more, you remain in an open, relaxed state.

Repeat this several times. For a few ins and outs of the breath, you might enjoy lingering with the chest lifted. Keep the neck free from strain as you explore opening up the chest and ribcage with gentle, full breathing.

Benefits:

The challenges of living and working in the world result in people universally rounding their shoulders and closing off the natural openness of the heart-center and the body. Let yoga help you move from a beaten-down feeling to that "get up and go" attitude that makes for business and personal success.

Invigorating this area with a few full breaths every morning feels absolutely great. This pose refreshes your lung capacity, helping with circulation and toning the whole system. It restores a quality of freedom and vitality to the entire body, clearing your head and leaving you better prepared to deal with the complexities of modern life. In short, it'll make you feel like a real "winner"—and that attitude will make all the difference in the day ahead.

Keyboard Warm-Ups

Imagine that the keyboard is your piano, the instrument on which you create beautiful music with the world. Like a concert pianist would, warm-up the fingers, hands, arms, and shoulders, with this series of stretches before diving in.

Interlace your fingers into a soft fist. Then stretch the fist above your head. Keep the fingers together, but turn the wrists up and open the palms to the sky.

Lengthen the arms even further skyward. Your gaze might be upward or straight-ahead—wherever you like as long as there's no strain. Lengthen your breath in and out as you stretch.

Then add some movement. Keep the fingers interlaced, but as you exhale, bring your soft-fisted hands behind the head. Breathing through your nose as you exhale, lengthen the arms up again.

When the arms are straight, draw your shoulder blades down the back. If you notice the shoulders coming up by your ears, relax them down again as you exhale. On the next inhale, you can restraighten the arms long, lengthening everything upward, then relax the hands behind the head on the exhale.

Variations:

While still seated, you might explore keeping the fingers interlaced and stretching to the side as you exhale. Take a moment, then inhale upright. Exhale to the other side. Change sides a few times.

Here's one more move: Keep the interlaced hands in the same shape, but lower them so that the arms are at shoulder-height. The arms move forward and straight away from you, with the palms facing away as well.

Notice that the arms will tend to pull out too far forward, causing a roundness in the chest. Adjust this by bringing the shoulder blades together on the back, lifting up the heart, chest, and ribcage. At the same time, keep extending the interlaced hands with a gentle vigor. After a few breaths, exhale and release.

Benefits:

A lot gets accomplished in these seemingly simple moves.

First, fingers get stretched. The hand and wrist—especially if you type at a keyboard all day—can really benefit from the lengthening.

By exploring the hands lifting above the head and then forward in front of you, you have a chance to really warm-up the shoulders and, once again, open the front of the body and heart.

Finally, moving side-to-side in the variation allows for a terrific stretch of the whole torso, lengthening it out as you invite the rejuvenating breath in.

As always, moving with an awareness of breath brings you closer to an integrated, calm, yet alert state of mind—perfect to launch you on the exciting ride of the day ahead.

MIDDAY
MAINTEN

ANCE

The order of the poses in this book is just one way of doing yoga. Remember that at its core, yoga is about "calming the storms of the mind."

So after you've sampled all the poses in this book, feel free to mix them up as you see fit. Your own experiences as you practice are definitely the best way to find the order and variations that work best to center you. In the end, what's most important is that you enjoy the exploration.

I've grouped these poses together because, as the day progresses, there are definitely moments when you want to revive. For me, that's usually before lunch or in the middle of the afternoon. You're not alone in experiencing a pre- or post-lunch energy slump. There's a biochemical basis for this, which is why many cultures incorporate an afternoon siesta in their daily routine at this time of day. Rather than reaching for that fourth espresso when you're tired, use these poses to help keep your energy high and your mind peaceful.

Corporate Toe-Pointing

So often, the world of office politics can be full of finger-pointing and back-stabbing.

In *Yoga for Suits* we're all about toe-pointing to warm-up the feet. (And rather than back-stabbing, we advocate back-rubbing to soothe achy muscles and a weary spine!)

Many people aren't sensitive to their feet (until there's a problem), but your feet really are your connection to the earth and being grounded, even if you're working on the 42nd floor of a skyscraper. Misalignment of the feet can affect knee problems and the spine itself. Fortunately, opening up the feet can be done in simple ways that are truly refreshing for the body and mind.

Slip your shoes off. Go ahead—the business world won't fall apart if you're in socks, stockings, or bare feet at your desk. No one needs to know.

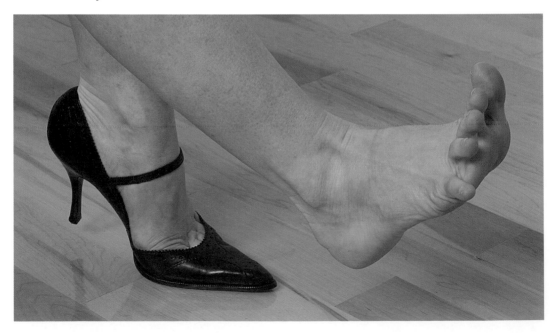

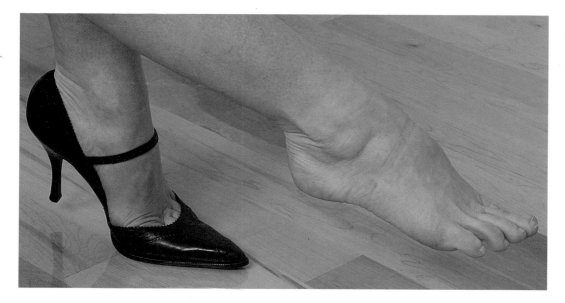

Most folks like to work with one foot at a time, letting the other foot touch the floor as the first is lifted from the ground. Some people enjoy moving both feet at once, particularly if they like a little added exercise for the abs by having both feet dangling off the ground.

Lifting a foot, rev it up by first pointing the toes back and forth, as though the foot were waving hello and good-bye. Really stretch the toes away and then flex them in toward your face. Especially for women who wear high heals and thus shorten their hamstrings, flexing the foot can be a truly important lengthening moment.

Next, circle the ankle in each direction, making a clockwise, then a counter-clockwise turn. Repeat this a few times.

Try spreading the toes wide apart, as well. Make as much space between each toe as possible.

Motivational speakers testify to the importance of having written goals, mission statements, and mottos. As another way of freeing up the foot, write something with the toes—anything. It could be a goal, a wish, a dream, or a *mantra*. A mantra is a sacred phrase or word—in Sanskrit or English or any language—that one repeats to stay focused. "Peace," "Freedom," and "Let Go" are all great choices. Find something that works to inspire you and use it. Free up your power to visualize through movement and breath-awareness.

Indeed, as you improvise your way through these or any other simple foot-opening moves, throw a little imagination into the mix. Take a mental vacation. Fantasize about cool grass in a perfect meadow. Enjoy a favorite beach memory of surf running through your toes. Close your eyes if you like, but absolutely watch your breath and invite it to deepen.

It may sound corny, but science backs up the power of visualizing. Often the brain can't distinguish between an actual experience and a vividly imagined one, so you can derive many of the stress-relief benefits simply by using your imaginative powers (rather than your frequent flyer miles).

Another way to look at it: Yoga is about taking this (and any) chance to free-up your mind—in this case, by freeing up your feet!

Benefits:

There's something incredibly refreshing about taking your shoes off—even if it's only for a few moments—and letting the feet breathe. Connect with your ideal vacation or your inner barefoot hippie if you want. Just like taking off your coat or hat, removing your shoes signals relaxation and ease.

Let yourself sink into that vast Asian tradition of being barefoot in sacred spaces, whether it be the temple or the home. (How much different office life would be if we were asked to invite some sense of the sacred into the workplace!)

Start here and now, taking this momentary break to loosen up so that the mind and spirit can run barefoot and free . . . then it's right back to work, but refreshed from your shoeless mini-vacation.

Spreadsheet Hip Opener

When tension isn't released from the body, it gets stored, for most of us in the hips and shoulders. Fortunately, even while seated, you can loosen your hips with a few gentle moves. Better still, this pose is so simple you can do it discreetly under your desk whenever you want to explore a little letting go.

You can keep your shoes on, but this is perhaps best done with them still off after your Corporate Toe-Pointing.

Gently bring one foot across the opposite thigh. Right away, you'll notice if this is too steep of an angle and not a great idea. As always, find the appropriate, pain-free yet slightly challenging position.

If the foot resists crossing the opposite thigh, simply bring it to the edge of the inner thigh. (One Note: Most folks find one side more open than the other, so notice that as well when you switch sides later on.)

Wherever the foot falls—across the thigh or to its inside edge—is just fine. Let the bent knee gently lower without putting any pressure on it. Sit for a few breaths as the muscles release. As always, sit tall and breathe deeply when doing these poses.

To intensify the stretch—and remember, that if your hips are tight, just sitting tall might be intense enough—explore bending forward.

First, come halfway down. You might rest the elbows on your bent leg—or on the top edge of your desk. This might be more than enough of a stretch.

If you're able and interested in taking it further, make sure you're far enough away from the desk that you won't bump your head, then allow the torso to ease further forward over the leg. Fingertips reach out in the direction of the floor. At the same time, try to keep your buttocks settled back on the chair, so that you stay nicely anchored and grounded in your seat.

Again, as with all yoga poses, what matters most is that you approach this slowly and calmly. Let the weight of the body draw you forward rather than trying to force anything. The feeling is one of melting into the shape, of softening by simply hanging out and letting gravity open up the hip.

Stay here for a few breaths and then switch sides, applying the same mindful approach.

Benefits:

Hips are an area of the body where many hold tension. When you spend countless hours sitting in your desk chair, your hips can get increasingly tight.

Letting the knee fall out to the side opens the hip. Bending forward intensifies this action, and lets the spine lengthen as well.

Be sensitive to yourself when you open the hips. It's not necessary to feel like you're being tortured to get a lot of benefit, especially over time with practice. Just hang out with a *reasonable* amount of sensation (not pain), breathing deeply and practicing gentle awareness.

Remember, you don't need to be sitting like the Buddha in a Lotus Position (that classic pretzel shape) to attain enlightenment—but still, why not take a few moments every now and then to let your hips unfold?

Wrist Upgrade

Seated a foot or so away from your desk, open your hands in front of you so that your palms are facing upward.

Place your fingertips on the bottom edge of your desktop.

Probably the thumb (and if you spread your fingers wide, maybe the pinkie) won't connect with the desk's bottom edge. Just the other fingers will, and that's fine.

While the fingers stay anchored to the desk, lift the wrist toward the ceiling and away from you. The fingers are now pointing downward. Do this gently, feeling the stretch in the hand, fingers, and especially the wrists.

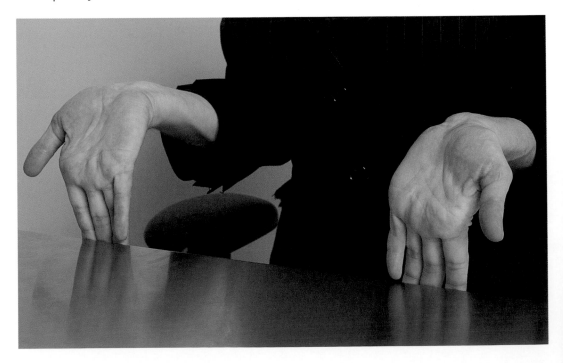

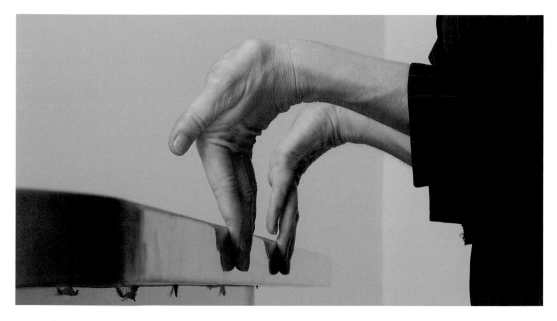

As the wrists reach upward with the inhale, so does the chest. As always, keep the shoulder blades softening down the back so that the heart and lungs can continue to open with each inhale and stay lifted during the deep exhale.

It's nice to connect this with a few full breaths, lifting the wrists on the inhale and lowering them on a gradual exhale. As always, moving gently and with real awareness is the right approach.

Benefits:

After long hours at the keyboard, the wrists can often suffer. More and more, Carpal Tunnel Syndrome affects countless people who live at their computers.

This pose is a counter-stretch (moving the hand in the opposite direction) and offers some kindness to the wrists to ease short-term strain and prevent long-term repetitive stress disorders. Spread this feeling of kindness, and when you return to the keyboard, remind yourself to extend that same spirit of kindness with every keystroke you write.

Banker's Pose

Here's another great way to stretch out the wrist and re-open the hands. It may seem a little funny—and bring back distant memories of a dance called "The Funky Chicken"—but your wrists and keyboard-cruising fingers will thank you.

Simply tuck your fingers under your armpits, leaving the thumb exposed and pointing upward.

As you exhale, gently draw the elbows back in toward your sides, allowing the subtle squeezing to release tension in the hand.

Remain for a couple of breaths, as though you were a proud banker with your thumb on your suspenders, celebrating a completed deal. Then release the hands smoothly.

Afterward it's good to do a counterpose, a complementary movement that frees things up in the opposite direction. This continual balancing of one pose after another, in harmony with each other but in opposite directions, is very yogic.

In this spirit, continue freeing up the muscles in the hands, by holding the palms in front of you for a moment while opening and closing the fists a few times. Notice the sense of relief you create whenever you open the hand after tensing it voluntarily.

As a next step, with each hand, explore the range of motion by circling the wrist around in every direction. Move slowly, but try many different possibilities of moving your hand around.

Benefits:

Too often, you can lose Big Picture focus, getting immersed in work at the keyboard, forgetting to break away, or vary your positions. Adding variety to your usual range of motion, helps allow repetitive stress to dissipate.

Applying a little pressure in Banker's Pose really does allow the wrists to open. Following this with some opening and closing of the hands and some gentle circling of the wrists is a great way to keep those keystrokes coming without strain.

Remember that life is about movement (both the body, the breath, and all those achievements on a healthy résumé); nothing is meant to stay stuck!

Victory Side-Stretch

If ever the day starts wearing you down, it's time to revive with a victory stretch.

As you raise your arms up high, palms open and fingers alive and reaching, enjoy a big inhale. Linger here, visualizing the big sale (the field goal as it were) or whatever victory inspires you.

Then exhale your hands together, fingers softly interlacing into a fist. The other fingers stay the same, as the two index fingers meet straight up (like a "church steeple" shape) to further lift the energy upward. Savor a few breaths here, lengthening up but at the same time letting

the shoulders fall on the back, melting away from the ears.

As you exhale, hands still in this shape, lean out to the one side, lingering for as many breaths as you like. Even though you're leaning to one side, try to weigh down the opposite hip as you stretch. Being anchored in your seat will really lengthen the entire side of your body. Then inhale as you return, upright and centered. Repeat on the other side, switching back and forth a few more times.

End by releasing the fingers but still holding the arms long and the palms open, and reach upward for several breaths. Let yourself enjoy the open feeling of the heart center stretching upward. Shoulder blades soften on the back to compliment the heart's opening skyward.

Exhale and lower the hands, refreshed and ready to return to the tasks at hand.

Benefits:

Stretching to the side adds length to the torso and stretches the spine.

Holding the arms above the head is a refreshing movement that opens the ribcage, allowing for better breathing. Holding your arms high also increases your heart rate and helps your circulation—ever wonder why symphony conductors live to such a ripe old age?

Adding to the physiological benefits, if you connect this uplifting gesture with a feeling of victory, satisfaction, and accomplishment, the visualization will have even greater effects on your movement and state of mind.

THE YOGIC OFFICE

Although we are definitely not our jobs, we usually spend a third to even half of our time at work. And although many elements of the work environment may be out of our control, there are lots of things we can do to brighten up the office experience.

The Organized Space

Check out some books and articles on *Feng Shui* (the Chinese study of interior design) to make your office friendly. First, you'll learn it's pronounced "Fung Schway." Then you'll find some tips that may prove right for you.

Create a Clutter-Free Zone

One thing that's definitely true for everyone is that clutter gets in the way of efficient productivity. You may be one of the rare types who claim to thrive in a messy environment, but it's more than likely you'll find a clutter-free workspace a boon. Besides making you lose time looking for things in the mess, the disorganized energy of clutter makes it harder to focus and stay on track.

Establish some basic rules for yourself. For example, try to touch a piece of paper only once: respond to it, forward it, file it, or throw it away. You might have a specific "Short Term" or "Current Projects" file—just make sure it doesn't become an out-of-control catch-all folder.

Besides encouraging clutter-control, Feng Shui also incorporates a lot of "vibey" advice that can sometimes work wonders. For example, having a small fountain in your office might have more of an effect than you think. The soothing sound of flowing water might provide the right background sound and feeling to allow you to remain more in the flow throughout the day.

Placement of Your Desk

Feng Shui consultants advise placing your desk so that it's not directly across from the entrance to your office. They also feel that you shouldn't sit facing a corner or the pointed edge of a piece of furniture. At the same time, your back should be near the wall in order for your mind to feel more relaxed.

Why not experiment a bit with the placement of furniture to see if this feels true for you and makes the office a more comfortable space? As with yoga poses, allow yourself the freedom to experiment with how things actually feel and work best for you, uncovering your own sense of flow.

Sitting Pretty

It's important to be comfortable in your chair. Make sure you can adjust the height and the arms so that you're sitting properly. Your arms should be parallel to the ground when your feet are flat on the floor. Otherwise, you might be putting unnecessary stress on the body, particularly your back, shoulders, and wrists. Online and in book stores, there are many good resources about ergonomics that can assist you in finding the most beneficial furniture for work activities.

Lighting

First, make sure there's enough light for you to see properly without any glare on your work.

Secondly, notice the kind of light your office uses; it can definitely affect your state of mind. Science has proven that workplace health improves and students learn better with the right lighting. Study after study shows that fluorescent lights, while seemingly efficient, have a draining, de-energizing effect on people. Full-spectrum fluorescent lights—those closest to natural sunlight—can ease your eyes by reducing glare, elevating your mood, and decreasing stress-hormone levels. Even if you can't rewire your building, adding a full-spectrum bulb to your desk lamp can help counter the harsh effects of overhead fluorescents.

Bear in mind that a deficiency of natural light, especially in the winter months, is often responsible for a form of depression known as SAD—Seasonal Affective Disorder. This is a very real condition (especially in the winter months) that fortunately can often be treated successfully with exposure to full-spectrum light.

At the same time, remember that outside light needs to be controlled by drapes or blinds to minimize computer screen glare. Make sure the angle of your terminal works for you. Bear in mind that filters on a computer screen can be helpful to reduce unwanted reflections. Even a shiny desktop—versus a matte or more darkly finished one—can be visually draining to the eyes.

Eye strain often builds up over time, causing headaches, irritability, and fuzzy thinking even if one isn't conscious of the problem. It's wise to take some steps to insure that your work environment doesn't become a sight for sore eyes.

Color Schemes

As every advertiser on Madison Avenue knows, color affects us on a deep and primary level. Individual response may vary—you may feel energized by red while I may feel it's gaudy—yet the significance of color shouldn't be underestimated.

If you can choose the color for your office, think about what associations and responses it provokes in you. Blue is thought of as calming and tranquil. Yellow clarifies the mind, orange stimulates creativity, and green has a healing, soothing quality. Even a splash of a favorite color here and there might provide the energetic boost (calming or enlivening) you require.

Music

Just like color, music affects us deeply. You may need to negotiate with fellow workers about their individual audio preferences, but most often something soothing in the background can enrich the atmosphere. This could range from calming classical to stirring light jazz, depending on the desired effect. If music isn't appropriate or possible for your office, you might consider a music break; enjoying a few choice tunes on your iPod could transport you out of the work world and make all the difference in your mood. (Don't, however, let yourself get caught dancing like Elaine on *Seinfeld*, unless you want your career to plummet!)

Good Scents

Okay, aromatherapy might seem like one of those crackpot ideas that's a million miles away from the bottom lines of American business culture.

On the other hand, the effectiveness of essential oils to create helpful brain chemistry is well-documented. Aromatherapy can help with many physical symptoms, particularly elevating mood and eliminating stress. Indeed, one study found that scenting an office with lavender reduced computer errors by 25 percent.

Again, a little sensitivity to your co-workers is in order—they might not be crazy about turning the office into a fragrant, tropical-smelling paradise of coconut and suntan oil— but a small scented candle, or a vial of pure herbal oils, might be enough to lighten the aroma in your immediate sphere.

Take a Deep Breath—maybe!

The Environmental Protection Agency estimates that 6 out of 10 buildings are "sick" and that indoor air quality is the United States' number one environmental health problem. A recent study by the U.S. Department of Agriculture found that ionizing a room led to 52 percent less dust, and 95 percent less bacteria, because many of the pollutants found in indoor air reside on floating dust particles. Fortunately, negative ion air purifiers are relatively affordable. If you suspect that your building is "sick," get one and then really breathe a deep sigh of relief.

Plants

More than just for Feng Shui or their simple beauty, plants freshen the air by adding oxygen to your environment. Even more importantly, new studies by NASA no less indicate that common houseplants do an excellent job of filtering the air for toxins and "sick building disease." Ivy, Chrysanthemums, Chinese Evergreens, and Philodendrons are just a few of these living, breathing air fresheners that can brighten your day while purifying your air against unseen toxins.

Early to Bed, Early to Rise

Sleep is central to good health. Make sure that you're getting enough each night. Studies in productivity consistently demonstrate that it's far wiser to work refreshed than to cram in endless hours behind your desk. (And if sleeping soundly is a problem, check out my book *Yoga in Bed* for lots of practical advice.)

Diet

Like sleep and exercise, a nutritious diet is one of the cornerstones of a healthy life.

Although it's sometimes tempting to binge eat when working late or under a deadline, simply put, you'll feel better (and work better) if you eat better.

If the temptation to load up on junk food is too strong, allow yourself some after you've had something substantial and healthy first. Like a strong cash flow, nutritious food provides the necessary energy and stamina you need to keep yourself productive and profitable.

Vacations

Everyone needs a little time off from work, preferably with little checking in and minimal back-burner attention to the office. In other words, a "true" vacation where you let your mind and body release from their usual tasks and challenges.

One wise Suit told me that his vacation officially began every time he made the decision and then committed (meaning he actually bought the plane tickets) to take time off. Indeed, the refreshing thought of that Utah ski trip or tropical cruise a month or two down the road can often make the rougher moments more tolerable. So take full advantage of whatever vacation possibilities exist for you. Beyond the pleasure of the time away, know that the vacation also enhances the quality of the time actually spent on the job.

In a way, this is very much in the spirit of yoga philosophy: A little surrender and release are necessary to balance the active and efforting side of things. So embrace the paradox: Take a vacation to become more productive.

WATER COOLER MOMENTS

Another yoga paradox: Sometimes when you're running behind, the most effective thing is to slow down a bit. Often a break may be the best way to move forward.

There's nothing like getting up and away from your desk to shift your perspective, even if it's just for five or ten minutes. Don't let yourself feel so tied down that escape is impossible. It's an office, not Alcatraz!

Here are some poses to do while standing up, before or after that much-needed trip to the water cooler, coffee room—or even that espresso bar across the street!

Climbing the Corporate Ladder

Standing up and, as though you were taking a giant step up the corporate ladder, place one foot (shoeless or not) on your desk chair. If your chair is on wheels, make sure it doesn't slide out from under you!

Take your opposite hand and bring it around to your knee. With one hand on the chair's back, twist in the direction of the bent knee, really standing tall and breathing deeply. See if you can incorporate some breath-awareness with the movement, going a little deeper into the twist on each exhale. Keep the bent knee stable on the chair, allowing it to provide some resistance as you twist against it.

After you finish a few breaths, inhale back to center and switch the foot on the chair. Repeat the same dance of the breath, the arms, and the movement, exploring the feeling of opening yourself up in every direction.

NOTE: Office chairs are different so you may need to modify this to work for you. What's key is that you feel grounded in your standing leg, that you breathe fully, and that you enjoy the movement of opening up through twisting.

Benefits:

This provides a great twist to loosen any kinks in the lower back and wring out any tension in the torso. The leg up on the chair really allows additional leverage to open up the body from a new angle, opening up the spine and toning the inner organs.

And, as always, the breath provides the way to move deeply and soundly into the shape.

Briefcase Bend

For some folks, touching their toes seems like a far-off—if not impossible—goal. Bending at the waist and coming forward can be a frustrating, even painful experience if the hamstrings (those muscles at the back of the legs) and lower back are tight. However, simply hanging over your legs is a tremendous way to lengthen the hamstrings and allow the lower back to stretch out nicely. Here are some ways to make it more approachable.

If the leg and back muscles are really tight, it's comforting to have something between you and the elusive floor. Your basic briefcase can serve a whole new purpose here, acting as a bridge between you and the ground.

Put your briefcase on the floor—on its short side, long side, or flat on the floor. Position it so that your fingertips can reach. Find a height that will allow your fingertips to touch the briefcase as you bend forward from a standing position. As you lengthen out over time, you'll notice that this position will change, with your hands going lower

briefcase will serve as an excellent reminder to do this stretch.

As you allow the weight of the torso to fall forward, keep the knees a little soft, meaning slightly bent rather than totally straight. If you soften the knees, you have a little more wiggle-room to play around with where the weight falls forward. When your knees are still soft, see if you can pull your weight forward over the center of the foot—this will lengthen the hamstring a bit more. If you like, you can play with gently straightening the legs, coordinating the motion with steady breathing.

Stay in the pose for several breaths. When it's time to come out of the shape, bring your hands to your hips. Inhale, soften the bend in the knees, and gently roll up to stand, head and neck last.

Sometimes if you come up too fast, or have stayed down too long, there's a chance of a little dizziness. Remember to do less next time, coming up more slowly as you steady yourself with a few simple deep breaths.

as your hamstrings stretch and your back releases. Of course, you can definitely improvise with something else—a phone book or two, a stack of files—but I think there's something about the steadiness of the briefcase that's particularly suited for this. In addition, the daily presence of your

To open up the shoulders even more, take your hands behind your back and interlace your fingers into a soft fist. Gently lift the interlaced fingers so that they travel toward your head, the shoulder blades meeting on the back. Let your forearms move toward each other. Linger here for several breaths, then release the hands, and (with soft knees) take an easy inhale on your way up to stand.

Benefits:

Everybody's hamstrings need a lot of frequent stretching. Men's hamstrings are often extremely tight, and women have the disadvantages caused by wearing fashionable shoes.

Besides stretching the leg muscles, Briefcase Bend really lengthens the spine. In addition, the internal organs such as the liver, spleen, and kidneys are gently toned.

Beyond this, all forward bends such as this one have a cooling effect on the psyche. The mind quiets if you let it, perhaps in gratitude for the changed perspective and the flow of fresh blood to the brain.

Downward Desk

One of the most classic yoga poses is Downward-Facing Dog. Yet scrambling around on all fours in the office might be a bit extreme, even for a liberal corporate environment. (Farther along, I have included a "Behind Closed Doors" chapter with some supine poses, just in case you should be lucky enough to have a door you can close, or an office where rolling around on the floor won't be frowned upon!)

You can get many of the benefits of the Downward-Facing Dog stretch, however, by approaching it from standing and using your desk.

Stand about an arm's length from your desk. Don't worry about measuring the distance—you can adjust it in a moment by walking a little closer or further away.

When you bend forward (keeping the knees a little soft), let your hands reach out for the surface of the desk. You want to be able to let the back straighten and flatten, as though it were an extension of your desk.

If you're too close to allow your heart and shoulders to melt downward—or so far away that your hands don't touch the desk—simply adjust where you're positioned.

Once you've found the right distance for that flat back, allow the weight of the head and chest to melt forward, dipping toward the ground. Pay attention to your breathing, allowing it to stay full and centered. The chest moves effortlessly with the flow of breath. Let the head go. Allow things to soften and melt.

Feel that the hips move away and behind you. Try to lengthen the spine. You can play with the knees being straight or a little soft to stretch the hamstrings at the back of your legs.

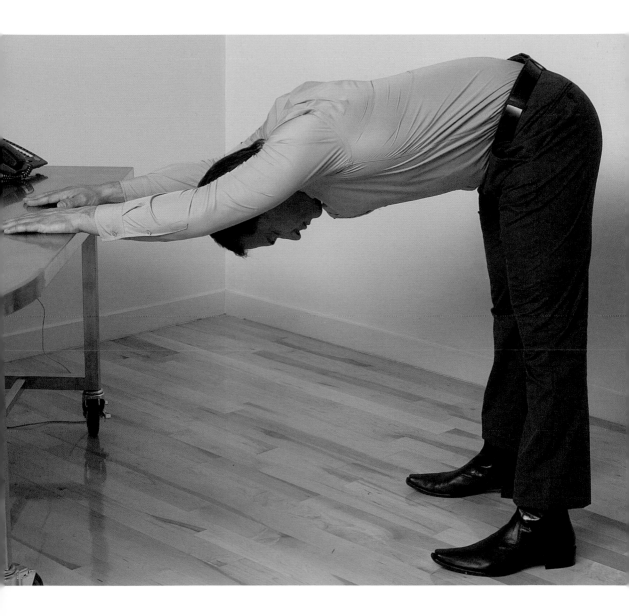

For many, the shoulders will feel this stretch most intensely. Stay with the breath as you lengthen the spine, dropping the heart and leveling the back. Let the head hang heavy, and either keep the gaze soft or simply close your eyes as you stretch.

Stay here for several breaths. Then soften the knees a little, and walk in toward the desk as you gently come up to stand. It's best to move slowly when you return to standing, especially if your head has been down for several breaths.

Benefits:

This stretches the legs, chest, and shoulders, letting you open the heart center during a round of gentle breathing. Hamstrings also get a nice stretch as you practice sending the hips away and lengthening the legs.

Besides the terrific physical benefits, there's also something calming, maybe even humbling, about this pose: It has the element of surrender built into it.

In yoga we're striving to achieve a balance of activity and peacefulness, of effort and release. In our culture, we're usually focused on, and therefore more comfortable with, the effort part of the success equation. Most often our society's formula for success involves endless, heroic effort. We feel compelled to always work hard, often trying to force things to happen.

In contrast, almost every yoga pose involves a sense of surrender and of letting go. Perhaps you can bring this part of the success equation into mind now. By releasing your brain and heart while touching your desk, you could also incorporate a few thoughts about softening any sense of struggle you have at work.

Most often our society's formula for success involves endless, heroic effort. Perhaps the part of the "Success Equation" you could bring into mind now is one of "Surrender," effectively gesturing to the universe that you've done your best and now you're letting go.

Truthfully, that's all any of us can do: offer our best and then let it go, trusting that the good efforts we generate will come back to us in ways we hadn't even imagined. *Karma* is a word often bandied about, but at its most fundamental level it means, *"The Universal Law of Cause and Effect."* At the end of the day, you've got to let go and trust that the investments you've made in hard work and effort will be rewarded. It's a universal truth that without surrender, there can be no peace of mind.

Seat of Global Exchange

In most of the world, squatting is the way people sit. We in the West rarely find ourselves away from a chair. For Westerners, sitting in a squat—even for just a handful of breaths—is a great way to open up tight hips.

When you position yourself against a wall, there's a great feeling of support, and the chance to lengthen out the back. You could certainly do this pose in the middle of the room, but having

some part of your lower back against the wall lends a feeling of stability.

To approach the pose from standing, simply bend your knees deeply, letting your tailbone sink down.

At the same time, keep lifting up your chest (rather than rounding into a ball).

You might find that your heels lift off the ground. That's fine. You can always place something under them (like the company directory) if you'd like them to be even, or just enjoy the deep stretch as they lengthen toward the floor.

Placing the hands in prayer not only helps to keep the knees widely spread, but also acts to open up the chest and lengthen the spine.

Hang out in the squat as long as you like, watching your breath for a few moments. Let coming up to stand be easy. While you could just inhale your way straight up, try straightening the legs as you bend over them for a moment, then gently rolling up, head and neck last.

Benefits:

Squatting is an excellent hip-opener, particularly for those who sometimes feel chained to their desks.

Personally, I've also found that squatting can also help relieve tension in the back, especially when I use a wall for support. When you let your hips fall open, while at the same time using the hands to remind the chest to lengthen upward, it greatly opens and releases tension. This makes it possible to return to your desk refreshed and ready to take on the world.

Rat Race Release

This classic runner's stretch is another excellent way to lengthen your hamstrings.

Standing about two feet away from your chair, raise your leg and place your foot on the seat. (If your chair's on wheels, obviously make sure it's not going to slide out from under you!) Bending at the waist, begin to lean over the straightened leg.

Make sure you've set things up so you can rest your hands on either the chair arms, or seat, or your nearby desk; in other words, as you're leaning forward, you're using the hands on a steady surface to help balance yourself, unless you're quite comfortable just reaching across the leg, as our model is.

Keep the standing leg alert (not locked, but not bent either) so that you have a solid foundation. Breathe steadily, letting your spine lengthen over the extended leg as you're bending forward. Linger for a good set of open breaths, and then switch sides.

Benefits:

Yoga is about seeing beyond the traditional rat race into what's really important. In other words, you can still run the corporate marathon, but you're released from any unnecessary strain and you reduce the risk of injury.

An intense hamstring stretch like this will open tight leg muscles, but with this and every pose it's the breath and awareness you bring to opening the body that really makes each day a winner.

Quad Quota

Standing tall, lift one leg off the ground and bend the knee. Reach back with the same hand as your bent leg to find the foot or ankle. Your other hand rests lightly on a steady surface to help you stay balanced.

Draw the bent foot in toward your buttocks, feeling the stretch in your quads. Remember to breathe deeply, inviting the foot toward you without forcing it. Stay tall.

Linger here for a few breaths as you enjoy the leg muscles lengthening, then switch sides.

Benefits:

A confident stride is important, so stretch out your quads as you stroll through your day.

Even if you can't escape the office for a marathon or a victory lap, your loosened legs will thank you!

Foot in the Door

Especially when you're starting out in the work force, you go through the proverbial struggle to get your foot in the door. Now that you've got the job, let the doorway itself open you up.

Stand not quite under the doorway, but a few inches before the threshold. Lift your arms so that the bent elbows jut out shoulder-height, like a saguaro cactus. Open the palms and place them on the edges of the door jamb, framing either side of the doorway. Then play with keeping the hands there as you gently tip the weight of the body forward, leaning so that your head and heart start to exit the room.

Go back and forth in the shape a few times. Try using the exhale to lean forward (bracing with the elbows) and the inhale to travel back into your office. Play with the rocking motion of the feet, too. All the better if you can slip off your shoes and really explore stretching the entire foot as you lean forward and back.

Absolutely hang out in the forward leaning for a few breaths, allowing the shoulder blades to move together and the chest to really open. Breathe deeply, maybe even sighing as the body and mind expand.

Lean into the future you want to create for yourself, your company, and the world.

Benefits:

This pose is interesting because you're using the weight and resistance of your own body to open yourself. Besides the tremendous benefits of expanding the shoulders and chest, you're also getting curious and playing with moving yourself against a counterforce—in this case, the body leaning forward versus the arms holding you in place.

In yoga we're learning not only to stretch physically, but also to apply the concepts of being balanced and centered in our lives, and working with opposition, not struggling against it. This shape allows you to explore the gentle tug of opening the chest against the groundedness of the legs, enjoying how the contrasting forces expand the body.

In the same way, the entire work world could be an exercise in opening up your mind and heart as you stretch, enjoying the challenges and responsibilities of your office environment. Who isn't pulled in different directions and tested daily by competing demands and conflicts? By staying grounded and yet leaning forward into work situations, you open yourself up while getting the job done!

Yogic Breathing

In the beginning of my yoga practice, I confess that I used to "tune out" whenever the teacher spoke about breathing. As a conventional workout guy, I thought it was enough to just "do the moves."

As I practiced more and more, though, I realized that everything my teachers were saying about the breath was true: Breathing properly—through the nose and deeply, letting the belly fill up on the inhale—was absolutely essential. More and more, changing my breath allowed me to go deeper into a yoga pose, and also provided the way to become more aware as I practiced. I've gone from viewing breath awareness as something extraneous—just New-Agey platitudes I could take or leave—to acknowledging that it is absolutely the greatest tool for opening the body, and for centering the mind.

Indeed, one of the many beautiful qualities of the breath is how powerfully and rapidly it can affect one's state of mind. Even a handful of breaths can transform one's consciousness.

This is particularly useful because often in the business world, it's necessary to quickly adjust your attitude. When the pressure is on—deadlines, demanding clients, and an assortment of Murphy's Law situations—the breath can be used to improve your mental state in mere moments.

Here are some of the most powerful breathing techniques available for your "Yogic Tool Kit."

Brain Buffer

This kind of practice is less about a physical workout than an energetic, mental clearing. By combining the energy of a physical gesture with the right mental visualization, you can sometimes move the proverbial mountain.

With yoga poses—as with anything—it's the state of mind that matters most. As a person progresses in yoga (or in a career), the work can become increasingly intense, therefore breath, attitude, and visualization become more and more important.

To practice it, just rub the heel of your hand against the space between your brows to generate a little heat. Not so hard, mind you, that you irritate the skin, but at the same time, enough to spark up a little bit of feeling. As you do this, you can imagine releasing tension or erasing a problem from your brain.

The space that you're rubbing is actually the third eye, a subtle energetic center in the body. There are seven main ones, called *chakras*. The chakras are a fascinating study in themselves, but for now it's enough to know that the third eye is considered a major location for your intuition. It's where you can clear up your internal vision—the part that allows you to really penetrate the "behind-the-scenes" stuff about life and work and all your personal and professional deals. As you spark the area with your breath and palm, let the possibility of real insight come into your life.

When you feel the moment's right, exhale the open hand away in a gesture of release.

With your third eye refreshed, you might imagine anything that's negative being wiped away as the hand moves from the brow. You could picture the gesture

as a good-bye wave to your problem, a mental house-cleaning through the gentle scrubbing of the palm.

Definitely keep the focus on your breath during this exercise and feel free to repeat the practice more than once. Some folks report a real sense of relief and release as they exhale the hand away. Others feel that through contact with this energy center, intuition improves. Almost everyone, however, feels that there's some clearing, cleansing effect when breath, visualization, and gesture combine.

Benefits:

A calmer mind. And with this calmer mind comes the freedom to allow an intuitive brainstorm.

Breath of Fire

As the name implies, Breath of Fire is a real pick-me-up.

Like almost every yoga breath, it's through the nose. Unlike most yoga breaths, however, Breath of Fire isn't meant to be long and deep. Basically, Breath of Fire is quick and fluttery—as if you were panting—but through your nose. It's a lot like rapidly sniffing in and out, but with a little light pulse in the belly.

Here's a good way to approach it. With your mouth open, try a few pants like a dog. Then shut your mouth and, breathing through your nose, continue the same rapid inhalations and exhalations.

Because this breath involves rapid contracting of the abdomen, it's great for helping to tone the belly through light pulses. For those reasons and others, however, it's not recommended for pregnant women. For pretty much everyone else, though, it's an excellent invigorator.

It is an intense breath, so a little light-headedness afterward is natural. That's why it's good to practice Breath of Fire in small doses (15-30 seconds to begin), followed by a few, back-to-normal deep breaths. You could add a second round if you like, or gradually increase the amount of time practicing it to a minute or two.

Benefits:

This is great for the lungs and a gentle toner for the diaphragm. This invigorating, energizing breath re-animates the entire system.

Rather than counting on that third triple espresso to keep you going (we *are* a coffee culture, but everyone should be careful about too much caffeine), when you need a quick recharge or a little extra office mojo—like right before that big presentation—explore Breath of Fire.

Balance Sheet Breath

Even if you're not an accountant, you no doubt understand the concept of a balance sheet where everything must add up and tally properly. In yoga, even more than in corporate bookkeeping, it's important to maintain an internal sense of balance, exemplified by even, steady breathing through both nostrils.

By switching the breath through the nostrils, you can center and calm your thoughts, evening out any cranky conversation between the right and left sides of the brain.

The description of this might make it sound more complicated than it is. Basically, you're blocking a nostril as you exhale, then inhaling on that same side. You switch sides every time you exhale. Here's how it's traditionally set up.

Your left hand rests on the knee. The fingers form your "A-OK" *mudra* of the thumb and index finger touching lightly with the palm open to the sky. (Mudras are hand-gestures that affect the mind/body connection in subtle but powerful ways. We yogis are resourceful folks, using everything at our disposal to practice the calm, yet alert state of mind we want to sustain.)

The right hand is going to do all the work. You'll use the thumb and ring finger (the pinkie finger hangs out with the fourth finger). The middle and index finger curl inward toward the palm. (If your fingers go astray into some other combo, that's fine. It's the quality of the alternate nostril breathing that's really most important.)

The right hand floats up and rests in front of your face. It'll stay in this position as you use the fingers to switch which nostril you're breathing through. Let's begin.

After a full breath, use the thumb to

gently block the right nostril as you exhale. Once you're empty, breathe in on the same left side. Close the left nostril with the ring finger. You're going to keep the right hand in place in front of the nose, and release the thumb to exhale.

Inhale on the same right side. Switch sides to exhale. Continue.

Inhale on the left side, then switch sides to exhale. Keep the rhythm going.

Inhale right same side. Switch to exhale. And so on.

One of the things about this breath that makes it a little challenging and therefore more effective, is that it takes a small dose of extra concentration. You have to focus on what you're doing mindfully in order to switch on each exhale. You can't "fall asleep at the switch." Rather, you're drawn fully into the task of observing yourself as you breathe more and more deeply. Once you find the rhythm though, it begins to feel quite natural.

It can be nice to close your eyes as you do this, savoring the completeness of the emptying out and the fullness of the inhalation.

It's also worth mentioning that invariably you will find that one side of the nose is more clogged than the other. Grab a tissue and blow freely if you find this is an obstacle to the practice. Realize that even in nostrils unaffected by colds or congestion, this favoring of one side is a natural phenomenon; in fact, the freer side will switch back and forth every few hours in the day.

There are even folks in India devoted to studying how this relates to different aspects of right/left brain communication and decision-making. There's no need to get obsessed with this, however. Just realize that the nostrils (like people themselves) have their own quirky changeability, and ride it out.

Continue for a few moments, then lower the hand and savor several complete, evened-out breaths.

Benefits:

Excellent for centering and calming your mind, this is both a restorative practice when energy is low, and a calming practice when feeling frazzled or scattered.

As an added bonus, alternate nostril breathing is a perfect "count to ten" break when tempers flare or when you need a self-imposed "time out" from the threat of workaday madness.

Digital Dancing

This is a practice designed to fine-tune the mind/body/breath connection on a subtle but deep level. It's also mentally fun and refreshing—like doing a crossword puzzle (if you like crosswords) or playing a video game. The rhythm and repetition create mental cruise control: The steady pattern isn't over-taxing to the mind but keeps it at a sustained level of alertness, requiring enough concentration so that it must be focused. It is like driving down a country road when you're relaxed enough to enjoy the scenery, yet alert enough to prevent dozing off behind the wheel. There's a yoga name for this kind of repetitive, focused practice; it's called a *kriya*.

Basically, this kriya is a dance for the fingers with the thumb. Beginning with the index finger and the thumb touching lightly, then the middle finger and thumb, followed by the ring finger and thumb, and then the pinkie and thumb. In other words, each finger has its moment to touch the thumb lightly, as the next steps in. Both hands perform these moves at the same time—although you might enjoy exploring one hand solo, as well.

Sounds are associated with the motion. "Sa-Ta-Na-Ma." "Sa" with the first finger and the thumb, "Ta" with the second, and so forth.

Over and over—fingers and thumb touch, as Sa-Ta-Na-Ma repeats.

Nowadays, with hobbies like knitting coming back into vogue, people are increasingly aware of the power of the dance of the fingers as a way to reconnect with an inner calm. The fluidity of the motion—like the chant of Sa-Ta-Na-Ma—has a cascading feel and draws you into its undulating rhythms.

The sounds are referred to as "Seed

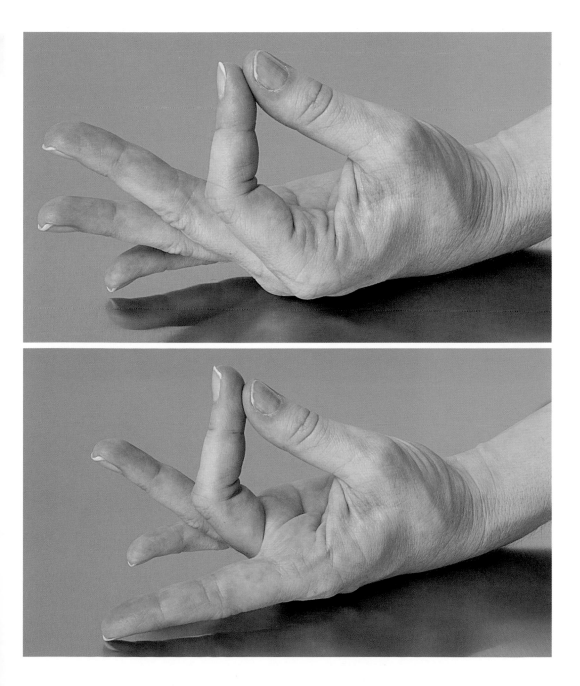

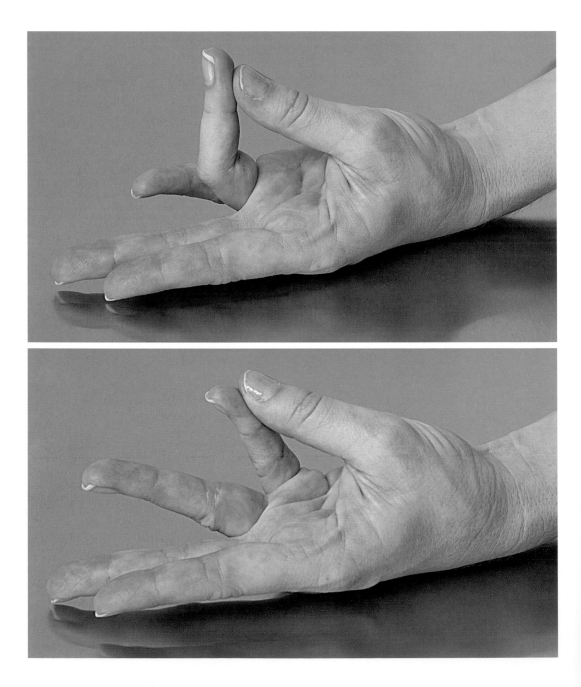

Syllables"—core sounds that have an effect in and of themselves. The sound is important, but you could repeat it mentally or just under your breath and get the exact same effect. (Frankly, you could even use an English word or phrase, if that feels better or more meaningful to you.)

Another possibility: You could try a one-handed version when you're on a phone call that's trying your patience or stressing you out. One hand holds the phone, the other hand dances; one part of you listens and agrees, another part repeats the mantra silently under your breath—especially for those times when you feel like muttering something else under your breath.

Make it your own, finding what works for you. After you try a few minutes of the repetition, notice what effect it has on your mood and attitude. Probably you'll find that once any resistance melts away, you can get lost in the repetition and rhythms, like you do when listening to a great jazz piece. When you finish, the world looks a little different.

Benefits:

Serious yogis have devoted lots of study to the subtleties of how nerve endings correspond to the dance of the fingers. The complexities in the body are profound, underscoring its interconnectedness with the mind.

Even without delving into all of this, the dance of the fingers can work its magic to free-up the consciousness by giving it a temporary activity, a time to play and relax through movement and breath. A few rounds of this kriya—even if it feels like, well, twiddling your thumbs—might just restore a little inner serenity before you realize it.

And in this digital age of multi-tasking, why not employ your dancing digits to do double-duty and soothe your mind?

BEHIND CLOSED DOORS

These four poses are great ways to relax. When it comes to removing tension from the body, they can help tremendously.

However, unless your office is super-relaxed to begin with, you might want to try them with the door closed. It's one thing to twist gently at your desk. Especially in more conservative business settings, it might be something else entirely to be discovered writhing on the floor!

Beyond privacy, these yogic moments are all about going inside, away from the world's demands. Therefore, definitely shut the door on the outside chaos and really allow yourself the pleasure of letting go.

Nest Egg

Lying on your back, draw bent knees into your chest. Hug them in gently, allowing your lower back to be stretched and released.

Some folks like to lift the head up to meet the knees. This is fine, as long as you don't feel any strain in the neck.

For most of us—especially if your hips are tight—it often feels best to cross the ankles, drawing the knees a little wider apart, but still deep into the chest.

Mind the breath, keeping it relaxed and long. Linger in this shape for a few moments. Release whenever you're ready, letting the feet touch the floor with the back still melted and long against the ground.

Benefits:

Opening up the hips while letting the lower back lengthen, this pose relieves major areas where people hold stress in the body.

And even though getting down on the floor might feel odd at the office, there's something grounding about it. Therefore, once you've shut the door, enjoy the feeling of reconnecting to the earth—even if you're fifty stories in the sky!

Bonus Baby

This pose is similar to Nest Egg, but I wanted to include it because sometimes even subtle variations make a difference. You might prefer one to the other, and this preference might switch depending on what your body needs on any given day.

 Lying on your back, bend your knees in toward the chest. Open the legs so they are hip-width apart. Then grab hold of the edges of the feet with your hands, opening the soles up so that they are parallel to the ceiling.

Draw your knees gently toward the armpits, breathing smoothly. At the same time, let your lower back release against the ground.

Again, this pose—like all yoga poses, frankly—should feel comfortable. Explore ways to make it work for you.

Some folks who are tighter in the hips find that rather than reaching for the edges of the feet, they simply let the arms fall on the backs of the upper thighs. (Feet are still parallel to the ceiling. It's the same effect— the weight of the arms draws the legs in toward the chest—but it's less stressful to attain.)

Or, like our model in the photograph, you might find that it's better just to cross the ankles and draw the knees wide out to the sides. While your feet won't be pressed against the sky, your hips will still open freely.

Sometimes a little movement might be soothing. You might rock a bit to the side or back and forth.

Nothing too dramatic. Just let yourself feel the openness you're creating in the hip and in the lower back as it releases.

This pose is often nicknamed "Happy Baby" in yoga classes. And like that Happy Baby, make sure it provides you with a great sense of relief and release. Gurgle if you must—remember, the door is closed!

Benefits:

Happy lower back and happy hips yield a happy body and content mind—the best bonuses of all.

Getting a Leg Up

Often we become so preoccupied with climbing the corporate ladder that we don't realize the benefits of turning things around. An inversion is any pose in which the heart is raised higher than the head. In yoga, these poses are considered both refreshing and calming.

First, lie down. You're going to swing your legs up the side of the most convenient, appropriate surface—your desk, some free wall space, a filing cabinet, or a sofa if your office has one.

I think the easiest way to come into the shape is to sit with your side quite close to the surface. Swivel around as you lift your legs, adjusting yourself as you need to.

For most folks, being reasonably close to the desk (or wall or file cabinet) will feel pretty good. You can shimmy yourself in or out as you like. It's totally not necessary to have super-straight legs, or to be right up against the surface. With yoga poses—like a favorite pair of jeans—having some softness to the shape is a good idea. You don't want the poses (or your jeans) to be so stiff or tight that you're uncomfortable. So do whatever feels most reasonable, especially since you want to linger here for a few minutes.

A pillow under your hips should feel nice. It adds a little support and gives your sacrum (the fused, triangular bone at the base of the spine, just under your waistband) some added support. The effect of this pose should be refreshing; you'll find that your breath starts to settle, and your thoughts along with it.

You can explore staying for several minutes, working your way up to five or ten.

As always, variations are possible. If you let your arms come above your head, you'll have more of a heart-opening, breath-

enriching experience. If they're by your sides, you'll have a more mellow journey.

Make sure that coming out of the pose is equally soothing. Start by removing any padding. Then you can soften the knees a bit as you roll to the side. Easy does it. Spend a moment sitting, and then you can stand up or try another one of these "Behind Closed Doors" poses.

Benefits:

You really have to try this pose for a few minutes to experience its effects. It may appear deceptively simple, but the benefits are truly real and verifiable.

Getting a Leg Up allows the circulation to be refreshed in the whole body. That creates a soothing effect for the brain. A pillow under the back can ease lower-back strain, and can assist in opening up the heart center, especially via lots of full breaths.

This pose is also a tremendous relief to the legs—particularly if you've had a long day standing or making a presentation. Taking the weight off them allows the blood flow to reverse and feels deeply soothing after a day of being and thinking "on your feet."

Finally, there's a psychological benefit as well. Explore flipping things around whenever you need a refreshing moment away from the daily grind. Again and again, it's thinking outside the box that solves corporate logjams. Going upside down a bit can do the same for you as an individual, taking you right back into the flow.

Moonlighting Twist

Twisting while lying on your back is extremely effective. With the back already released on the ground, there's an ease and gentleness to this move that's pure pleasure.

Approach it this way. First hug the knees into the chest for a moment, then let them drift to one side, lightly stacked on top of each other. Arms open wide into an easy T-shape.

Try to let each shoulder blade fall to the ground. If the shoulders are heavy and resting, the hips can fall further away as you linger in the twist. In other words, allow gravity to keep the shoulders dropping to the ground, and the hip will gently curve away in the shape. You can even lightly weigh down the twisting thigh with your hand, applying not so much pressure as just a subtle reminder to open and soften away.

After a few breaths on one side, inhale and draw the knees together, back into the center.

Move over to the other side in the same way. Let the bent knees fall in the other direction, arms also T-shaped and open. The head and the gaze are directed away from the bent knees so the neck can release and relax. Linger here and then either inhale back to center, or switch back and forth a few times.

You might enjoy the movement from each side, flowing back and forth over several breaths. Or perhaps lingering for a few moments will be the perfect prescription for your peace of mind.

Benefits:

This pose creates a gentle release for the lower back and a lengthening of the side of the body.

Given how high-pressured office life can be, why not take this great opportunity to roll around on the floor for a minute or two and let the mind wander free!

WINNING WIND-DOWNS

Most Suits don't keep office hours based on the proverbial factory whistle, but everyone feels the grind when it comes down to the homestretch.

Here are end-of-day moves that can give you a little more stamina to complete your tasks and simultaneously allow you to close up shop for the day, leaving accumulated stress behind.

The Eyes Have It

Almost any job that requires looking at a computer screen or reading documents can cause a real strain on the eyes.

Definitely explore all the lighting advice offered on page 53 in the chapter, "The Yogic Office," and be sure to absolutely try these eye exercises.

As you inhale, let your gaze drift upward, as though you were looking at midnight on a clock. As you exhale, keep your head steady, letting the eyes drift smoothly down to six o'clock. Inhale your gaze up to midnight, then exhale back down to six o'clock a few times. Repeat a few times.

Continue in this way with a horizontal pattern from three o'clock to nine o'clock—again, it's the eyes that are moving, not the head or neck. Coordinate the inhale with one direction, then exhale back. Explore this several times in each direction.

After you've done these movements, slowly let your eyes drift in a full circular motion, pausing at each number on your imaginary clock-face. In other words, look at one o'clock, pause for a beat, then move to two o'clock, three o'clock, and so forth. When you reach midnight, switch and travel with your gaze counter-clockwise. Go at a steady, reasonably slow pace, making sure your breath is smooth. After you've finished each direction once or twice, close the eyes softly to let them rest completely.

Benefits:

With these exercises you'll not only strengthen your eye muscles, but also increase your concentration.

Often our eyes tend to "grip" things they see, adding to the sense of strain. When you close your eyes after these movements, really let the eye muscles release, allowing a feeling of the eyes

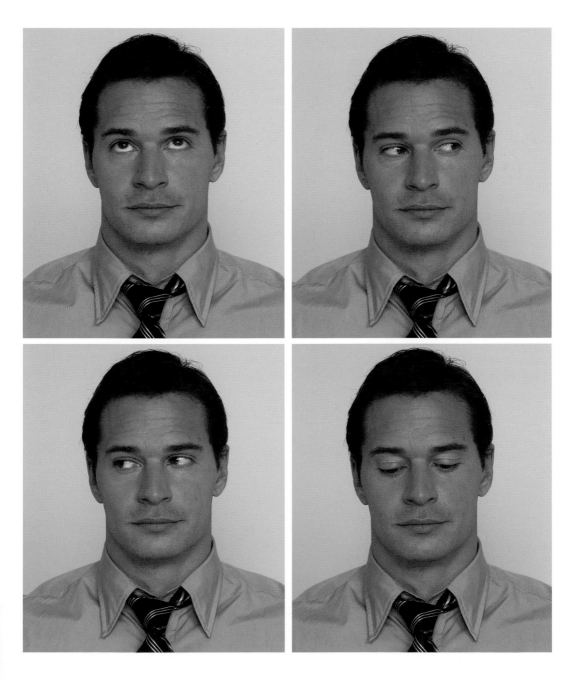

drifting back into the sockets. You'll ease not only your vision, but also your mind.

As you move your eyes slowly in each direction and then circle and counter-circle, you'll find yourself taking stock mentally because you're slowing down the stimulation to the brain. With simple, subtle movements and coordinated breathing, a soft kind of concentration arises that takes place without any force in it.

And that's what yoga is about: focus without strain, alertness without tension.

Mental Maneuvers

When you're sitting at a desk all day, working at the computer, or making phone calls, your head, neck, and shoulders are prime targets for accumulating tension.

Here's a trio of moves to release these weary pedestals for your frazzled brain.

Neck Circles

When circling the head around, move the neck mindfully. Especially in the beginning, it's nice to exaggerate the slowness, allowing the head's weight to fall and bob as you begin some gentle rotations.

I personally prefer half-circles rather than going all the way around, especially when starting this series. I like to linger with some half-circles in the front, swaying the head a few times gently in each direction as I watch my breath.

Let things deepen on each round, moving the ear and shoulder closer together on each pass, allowing the head to roll heavily forward.

Then explore circling the head toward the back. As always, stay deeply aware of the breath.

After a few times in each direction—again, always moving smoothly and staying mindful of the breath—try a few full rotations. After several circles in each direction, inhale the head back to center.

Shoulder Shrugs

Inhale your shoulders up by your ears. Lower them down as you exhale. Repeat several times, perhaps letting the shoulders linger in the shrugged-up position for several breaths before exhaling them down.

Shoulder Circles

Raise the shoulders high and then lower them as they roll forward, down, and back. Continue this rolling motion, finding your own breath and coordinating with the movement.

Repeat the motion in the opposite direction, lifting the shoulders up, then rolling them back and down.

Switch directions a few times each way, allowing the entire torso to benefit from the steady but invigorating breath and movement.

Benefits:

The neck and shoulders are prime areas of stored tension in the body, particularly for the desk set. Gently exploring movement and breath can unkink the neck and relax the shoulder blades.

Most importantly, releasing physical tension in these areas can re-establish clear thinking and an evenhanded mood. It's this mind-body connection that yoga explores and deepens, allowing you to find a calm center even in the whirlwind of office life.

Big Picture Vision

Rub your palms together as though you were trying to warm them over a campfire. Do this for about ten seconds or so, working vigorously enough to generate a little heat.

Rest the warmed palms over the closed eyes, without putting any pressure on the eyelids. In fact, it's probably best to have the open palms hover just above the skin, allowing the heat to sink in and relax the eye muscles.

Savor a few breaths with your eyes closed. As your eyes soften, a few deep breaths can allow you to gather and refocus your thoughts.

Keeping the eyes closed, see if the skin at your temples can also soften a bit. As the relaxation spreads over

to the rest of your face, let the jaw slacken. Notice if your teeth are clenching, then allow some space between the back molars.

As you remove the hands from your face and gently open your eyes, notice the softness and calm that you've created. Realize this state is almost always only a few breaths away.

Benefits:

Eyestrain is a dangerous side effect of doing business in the modern office, especially with computer glare and reading fine print.

Relaxing the eyes—and, more importantly, softening one's attitude and inner mindset—are necessary components for healthy inner and outer vision.

Having a "Big Picture Vision" is important for any company or individual's success. It's all too easy to get bogged down in the details and lose the more important goals one has. That's why staying centered and relaxed through poses and practices like these is so vital toward preserving the "Big Picture Vision" of a happy, productive life.

Brainstorm Booster

Breathe in deeply. Then, starting at your hairline, rub your fingers through your hair. Eyes can be open or closed, but keep the breath very full and the focus on the sensations of the fingers massaging the scalp. Let the hands roam all over your head, covering everything as they move back and around, until they find the nape of your neck. Repeat a few times, varying the pressure, or even perhaps adding some gentle scratching moments.

Add to the effectiveness of this movement by throwing in the visualization of your choice. You might imagine that you're washing negative thoughts away, or perhaps that you're kneading away the kinks in your brain, much as a masseur might massage your back.

If you're feeling uninspired or sluggish, you might imagine that you're enlivening your brain with flashes of brilliance. Or perhaps rubbing some magic into it, as though the skull were a crystal ball.

Simply allow yourself the fullness of the experience of your hands in contact with your scalp so that you can access an interior, two-minute vacation.

Even one minute of this deeply-breathed, keenly-observed motion of the fingers over the scalp can shift your perspective. That's truly the magic of yoga: the possibility of transforming your thoughts and experience through breath/body awareness.

Benefits:

Besides the fun of fantasizing that you're starring in a shampoo commercial, a few moments of tactile contact combined with breath awareness can help shift your mental state.

By changing the focus from everything that's going on outside yourself—the ringing, flashing phone lines, the paperwork that's piling up—to an interior awareness of skin, scalp, and most importantly, the breath, you regain peace of mind.

117

Thought Massage

Done consciously, rubbing at the temples can be as soothing as a massage to the brain itself.

It's fun to find the right touch with the heel of the hand, (or perhaps using the finger tips). Personally, I like the heel of the hand, although you might prefer the lighter touch of the fingertips. The level of intensity that's right for you is something highly personal, and varies from individual to individual. A little pressure tends to be helpful, but you don't want to rub so hard that you irritate the skin. The tempo should definitely be slow and soothing.

You might start with the eyes closed and the head dipped low. As you're rubbing lightly, however, see if you can lift the head slightly, feeling the chest open more fully with the breath. Your eyes are still closed, but you're softening and opening up inside.

Bring your breath into your awareness. Let it lengthen and deepen as you explore the circular rubbing, switching directions as you wish.

While rubbing my temples, I imagine the breath also moving through the whole of my spine, from its very base at my tailbone to the crown of my head. Rubbing the temples allows my focus to really be interior, and I imagine waves of energy moving in each direction.

Benefits:

Conscious breathing works miracles to reduce stress.

Use this practice of rubbing the temples to reconnect with the whole of the breath, stretching the flow as long as possible with every inhale and exhale.

You'll find that having reconnected with breath and touch even for a few moments, you're ready to once again focus calmly and clearly on whatever business problems, stacks of papers, or ringing phones demand your attention.

Necktie Rubdown

Loosen the knot of your necktie (that is, if you're wearing one). Open the top collar button of your shirt or blouse. Let your fingers find the back of your neck. Elbows lift up as the fingers point down. Allow the hands to gently dig in and soothe those aching neck muscles.

You may be surprised when you find how tense this area actually is. Really knead the muscles here, allowing the massage to go as deep as you like.

Let your thumbs thoroughly explore the neck, shoulders, and collar bones as well. Let the head drop a bit and hang heavy as you work your fingers over the entire region of your neck and shoulders.

Benefits:

A looser, kink-free neck paves the way for a freer, unclogged brain. Time and again, it's simply by re-establishing the mind-body connection that a boost of fresh enthusiasm arises for the tasks at hand.

Closing Up Shop Twist

This is the third twist I've included in this book. Why? Because twisting is so terrific when you're seated at your desk at the beginning, middle, and end of your workday, that I felt I should offer several different variations. Here's a highly effective twist that—like all these poses—you could do anytime.

Rather than facing straight ahead, just swivel over so you're sitting on the side edge of your chair.

Inhale yourself up tall. Then reach behind you toward the back of your chair, probably resting your hands on the top area or framing the headrest.

The beauty of this variation is that you will use your hands on the chair's back as you twist. As you exhale, twist toward the back of the chair. Repeat this a few times, being careful not to strain the neck.

As always, it's good not to force the twist in only one direction. When you inhale, it's nice to back away a bit from the twist and get taller, while the exhale allows you to go further into the twisting movement. Following the current of the breath this way allows you to open more deeply into the twist without straining and, at the same time, connects awareness to your body, breath, and mind.

Swing on over to the other side and repeat.

Benefits:

Twisting loosens the spine, especially releasing tension in the lower back. In addition, it wrings out all the internal organs, rejuvenating them with fresh blood, as it rejuvenates the whole body.

Enjoy the beauty of the twist itself, and the symmetry of beginning and ending the workday with this refreshing exercise.

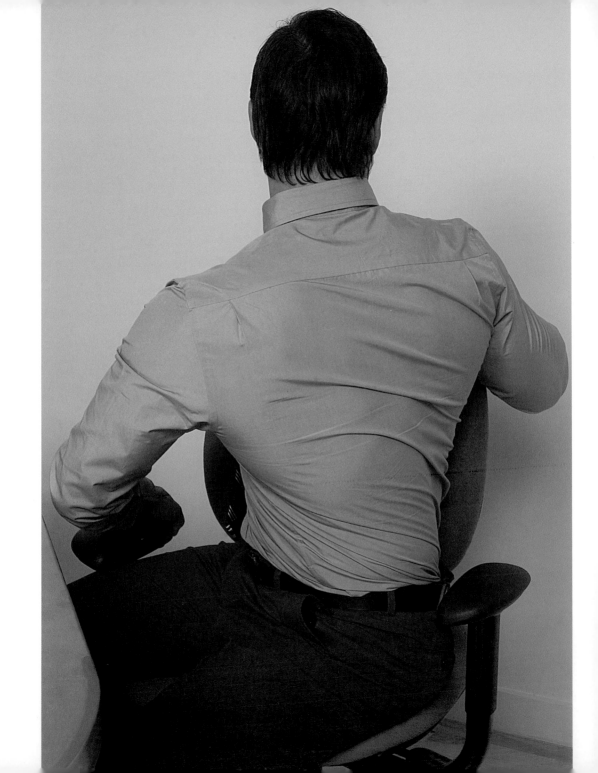

Remember: It's great to keep "checking in" with yourself as you work, maintaining an awareness of your physical and mental states as part of the picture. So many outside forces demand your attention—co-workers, clients, assistants, emails, memos, and deadlines, just to name a few—that maintaining an inner awareness can get lost in the shuffle unless you bring it to the forefront.

By having a consistent practice of yoga moves and breath breaks, you can forge some space in your schedule to stay attuned to your own needs. These moments of increased calm and self-awareness of your interior state will spill over and benefit you and your work universe in ways that will pleasantly surprise you. Framing the day with this simple twist (or any other pose you respond well to) is a great way to establish a kind of physical symmetry into your *Yoga for Suits* practice.

Clear Your Desk Meditation

Before I started teaching yoga full-time, one of my jobs was writing and producing for a Japanese TV network. Several employees would end each day with a ritual of clearing off their desk, gently cleaning the surface with a little Windex and a paper towel. It's not that their desks

were physically dirty—although I was sometimes surprised at how much New York City dust and grime would appear on the paper towel! It was much more of a one-minute cleansing ritual that let them complete the day.

Try it. Even if you need to leave paperwork on your desk, you could start by simply restacking and adjusting things. Then take a brief swipe with a paper towel and some cleaning agent. Trust me: Something about your desk space will just feel different: cleaner, fresher, and stress-free.

Of course, the most important thing is the mindfulness with which you do this. Simply affirm the thought that you're finishing up for the day, leaving work behind, ready for a fresh start for tomorrow. See if you can truly leave the day's trials and tribulations rather than taking them home with you.

I say create any ritual that works for you: turning off the computer (and backing up your data!), saying goodnight to the security guard or the office cleaner, or feeding your office goldfish. Establish a gesture that says to your brain, especially to your subconscious: The workday is over. I'm letting everything go for now.

This meditation—like all the daily practices you read about in *Yoga for Suits*—helps you achieve and recreate a productive, creative, refreshed state of mind that's designed to work for you.

In business, corporate types often talk about "the bottom line." And—although I'm no M.B.A., I know this means a hard look at the end result of any business endeavor's profits and losses.

When it comes to life, however, the "bottom line" is peace of mind. It's about being happy, and—if not always in blissful nirvana—at least calm and coping, no matter what the storms of life throw your way.

Working with your Yogic Toolkit is the best way I know to raise the bottom line of your life from frustration to acceptance, from frenzy to calm. And in or out of your business suit, that kind of profitability seems like the smartest move you can make.

MISSION STATE-MENT

Work is love made visible.

—Kahil Gibran

If only . . .

So often work can mean drudgery or a waste of time. Punching the clock. Running 9 to 5 on a treadmill. It's all too easy to think of work as just the price you pay to survive.

How amazing it would be if we could transform our attitudes towards our livelihoods. It's my hope that *Yoga for Suits* might just be a way to begin.

Again and again, I've stressed that yoga is not just about the physical poses. It's about attitude and outlook. Thus, there's often no better or more challenging a place to practice yoga than in the office.

I know the idiot's warehouse
Is always full.

—Hafiz, fourteenth century Sufi mystic and poet

Work is the ideal setting workshop to practice everything yoga's about: being calm and centered, living with principles, staying tuned in to the body/mind/spirit connection. Indeed, the Buddha spoke about freeing the mind from grasping and attachment. What more perfect place to practice the challenges of compassion and honesty, striving without aggression, and balancing effort with surrender?

Let the beauty we love be what we do.

—Rumi, thirteenth century Sufi mystic and poet

In the end, seeing your job not just as a paycheck but as a conduit toward helping enrich the lives of others (including yourself and your family) is one way to start.

Almost every job provides some kind of product or service that benefits the world. During the moments when things are most frustrating, perhaps you can see that whatever you're doing will be of some useful value to someone else. Sometimes a few moments of this kind of recollection—remembering your personal mission statement, as it were—can bring some yogic calm into your life.

It's my hope that with this book, the timeless practice of yoga will find its way into our offices and help its readers (suited or not) in the universal quest for a more meaningful, happier, and productive life.